PIRANHAS

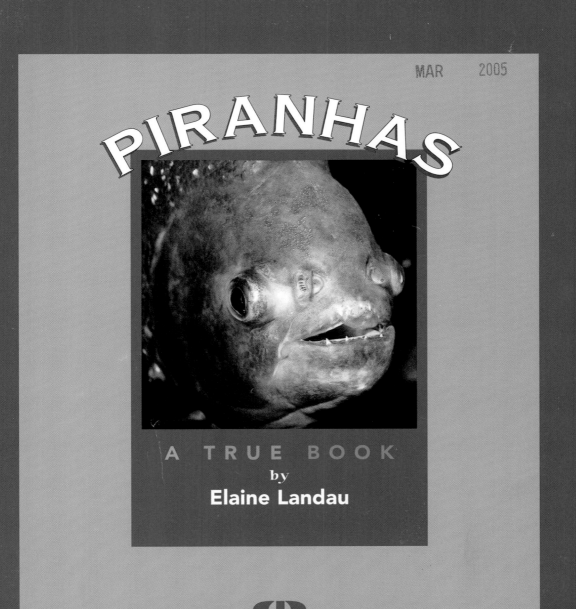

A TRUE BOOK

by

Elaine Landau

Children's Press®
A Division of Grolier Publishing
New York London Hong Kong Sydney
Danbury, Connecticut

Reading Consultant
Linda Cornwell
Learning Resource Consultant
Indiana Department
of Education

A girl views
a piranha

Visit Children's Press® on the
Internet at:
http://publishing.grolier.com

Library of Congress Cataloging-in-Publication Data

Landau, Elaine.
    Piranhas / Elaine Landau.
        p.   cm. — (A True book)
    Includes bibliographical references and index.
    Summary: An introduction to the various species of fish called pira-
nhas, discussing their reputation as killers, their physical characteristics
and habits, and their suitability as pets.
    ISBN: 0-516-20673-7 (lib. bdg.) 0-516-26498-2 (pbk.)
    1. Piranhas—Juvenile literature. [1. Piranhas.] I. Title. II. Series.
QL638.C5L35   1999
597`.48—dc21   98-16117
                                                                    CIP
                                                                    AC

GROLIER
PUBLISHING

Contents

Piranhas are among the most feared fish in the world.

Piranha!

When most people think of a piranha (puh-RAH-nah), they think of a savage, blood-thirsty fish.

Can a group of piranhas really strip an injured croco-dile of its skin and flesh in just a few minutes? Can they turn a human swimmer into a pile

The smallest amount of blood will attract piranhas.

of bones in about the same amount of time? Does the scent of blood in the water send piranhas into a feeding frenzy?

Yes. All of those statements are true. The piranha is a fierce freshwater predator that is found in the rivers and lakes of northern South America.

The Amazon is the world's second-longest river. It is about 4,000 miles (6,000 kilometers) long.

(A predator is an animal that hunts other animals for food.) Many piranhas live in the Amazon River Basin. The Amazon River Basin is the area of land that surrounds South America's Amazon River. However, the stories we hear about these "killer fish" are often worse than piranhas really are.

The word "piranha" does not refer to a single type of fish. It refers to a group of

Red piranhas, one of the twelve species of piranhas

about twelve species, or
types, of fish. Some species
of piranhas are deadlier than
others. This book will tell you
what piranhas are really like.

A Piranha's Life

A piranha doesn't look like a savage killer. Most piranhas are olive-green or blue-black. Some species have spots or stripes along their sides. Others have red or orange bellies.

Piranhas are not very big fish. The average adult piranha

A blue-and-black-colored piranha (above) and a red-bellied piranha (right)

is about 8 to 12 inches (20 to 30 centimeters) long. However, some types of piranha grow to about 22 inches (56 cm) long.

These young piranhas will grow to be about 8 to 12 inches (20 to 30 centimeters) long.

You can spot the more dangerous kinds of piranhas by the shape of their head. The deadliest piranhas have a rounded profile. (A profile is a side view of the head.)

The round shape of the profile of these piranhas (left) indicates they are one of the more dangerous species. The small jaws on these white piranhas (right) are a sign that they are not as dangerous as other piranha species.

They also have larger and stronger jaw muscles than other piranhas. The less fierce piranhas have a groove just above their eyes.

13

Piranhas are probably best known for their jaws and teeth. They have a lower jaw that sticks out past the upper jaw. All of these fish have thick lips. But the teeth of various species are arranged differently. However, every piranha has a mouthful of razor-sharp teeth. These teeth can cut through flesh quickly. The piranha's jaws have sometimes been compared to animal traps that tear through an animal's limbs.

The piranha's eyesight is not too good. But in the muddy waters of its world, eyesight is not as important

Piranhas do not need to rely on their eyesight in the unclear waters of their habitat.

as other senses. These predators have excellent hearing. They also possess a strong sense of smell. They are extremely sensitive to any vibrations or movement in the water. They have an amazing

ability to detect the presence
of an injured or dying fish—
even from a distance. And,
despite the muddy waters, the
piranha's highly developed
sense of smell allows it to track
the blood from other fish.

Piranhas' sense of smell is so
advanced, they can detect as little
as two drops of blood in the water.

Hunters

Piranhas spend most of their lives with a school, or group, of other piranhas. The number of fish in the group depends on the type of piranha. It also depends on the area it comes from. Piranhas often travel in a pack along rivers. They search for food and attack their prey

A school of piranhas

as a group. They have been
known to bite one another
as they excitedly devour
their prey.

As one piranha devours a chunk of meat, the piranha in the background stays a safe distance away.

As long as there is enough food for all the fish, piranhas do not actually eat each other. This only occurs in the wild, when food is scarce. When this happens, the larger members of the group have an advantage over the smaller ones. Piranhas that are kept in overcrowded aquariums also have been known to attack and devour each other.

Most public aquariums are careful not to keep too many piranhas in the same tank.

A piranha waits among plants and rocks for a possible meal to swim by (top). A piranha can move so quickly that the only sign that an attack has taken place is its mouthful of meat (bottom).

In their natural environment, piranhas do not always hunt for prey in groups. Sometimes they stalk and attack victims on their own. In these cases, the piranha may wait quietly behind a rock or a plant until just the right moment. Then when a school of other fish swims by, the piranha grabs one of them. The attack is usually so fast and sudden that the other fish in the school might not even know what happened.

Piranhas and People

Many scary stories are told about piranhas devouring humans. There are also stories about piranhas tearing off the arms or legs of a swimmer or a fisherman. But many of these stories are not true. Although piranhas have been known to kill humans, they prefer to eat fish.

Most people (such as this scuba diver investigating a porcupinefish) are not in danger of being attacked by piranhas.

The only time piranhas are a real threat to people is during a drought. A drought is a long period of time when the weather is very dry. During

As long as this South American river remains full of water and other fish, the piranhas that live here will not be interested in attacking humans.

these times, the lakes that the piranhas live in begin to dry up. By then, the piranhas may have already eaten all of the available fish. Attacking a swimmer may be their only way to survive. But in rivers that are well stocked with fish, piranhas have passed up fishermen who were waist-deep in the water.

Of course, people who fish for piranhas risk being bitten as they handle their catch. Many bites can occur when piranhas struggle to get away and come in contact with the

unfortunate fisherman's fingers. However, these fish are considered quite tasty. They are commonly eaten by the people living near the Amazon River Basin.

More Than Food

An Indian hunter in the Amazon rainforest

Piranhas are more than just a source of food for the rain forest Indians of the Amazon River Basin. For example, the Tucuna Indians use piranha teeth as decorations. They also use them as razors or for cutting. The Indians catch piranhas using fishing rods, fishing nets, or by shooting them in shallow water with bows and arrows.

Many of the Indians of South America's rainforest travel and fish in dugout canoes.

Killer Pets

Until about twenty-five years ago, piranhas were not kept in home aquariums. You had to go to a public aquarium or a pet store to see one.

Today, many people want unusual pets. Some people keep piranhas because they enjoy having a "killer pet" to

Only people with a lot of experience keeping fish should own a piranha.

show their friends. However, piranhas are definitely not for young aquarium keepers— or even for inexperienced older ones.

Keeping a piranha is not easy. These fish need large tanks. Some of the larger species of piranhas may require tanks that hold up to 100 gallons (400 liters) of water! Since most pet stores or aquarium shops do not carry tanks that big, a special container might have to be built. Then the owner must check the building plans for the home. When filled with water, such a large tank might be so heavy that it would crash through the floor!

Many species of piranha, such as this silver piranha (above), grow too large to be kept in home aquariums. The fish tanks (right) that are usually found in pet stores are not big enough for the larger species of piranhas.

There are other things to think about before buying a piranha. Check the laws where you live. In many states, it is

It takes research and careful planning to have a home piranha aquarium.

against the law to keep a piranha in a home aquarium. And even if state laws permit it, local (town) laws sometimes forbid it. Officials can not be sure that everyone who owns a piranha will act responsibly.

There is another problem that occurs with keeping pet piranhas. As these fish grow larger, some owners may feel that their piranhas have become too costly to feed and to care for. Or, they may simply get tired of their ferocious

Although piranhas don't have to eat live food every day, it can be expensive to stock up on supplies of piranha food, such as these gold fish.

People are concerned that unwanted piranha pets would destroy the fish already living in certain waters.

fish. As a result, officials are concerned that people may dump unwanted piranhas into local waterways. The piranhas could destroy the delicate balance of fish that exists in rivers and lakes. It is also feared that the piranhas could be a danger to swimmers.

A Piranha Mystery

Scientists and wildlife officials argue that it would be cruel to the unwanted piranhas to release them into waters in the cooler areas of the United States. They stress that fish from tropical areas have always lived in heated aquariums. Piranhas are tropical fish.

These red-bellied piranhas live in the tropical waters of South America (top). This thermometer (bottom) in a piranha aquarium shows a water temperature of about 78 degrees Fahrenheit (25 degrees Celsius). This is just right for tropical fish.

They would freeze to death if they were dumped in water that is too cold.

The scientists' and officials' argument makes sense. But something very strange has already occurred in a few states in the midwestern area of the United States. A number of piranhas have been

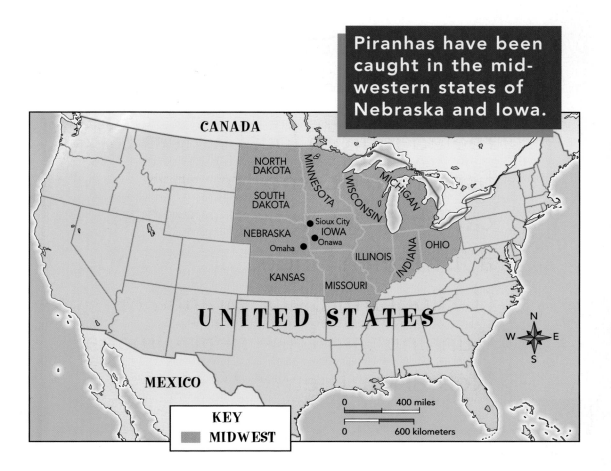

Piranhas have been caught in the midwestern states of Nebraska and Iowa.

CANADA

NORTH DAKOTA

MINNESOTA

WISCONSIN

MICHIGAN

SOUTH DAKOTA

NEBRASKA

Sioux City
IOWA
Onawa

Omaha

ILLINOIS

INDIANA

OHIO

KANSAS

MISSOURI

UNITED STATES

MEXICO

N
W E
S

0   400 miles

0   600 kilometers

KEY
MIDWEST

A black piranha, similar to the one that was caught in Cunningham Lake

reeled in from local waters by fishermen hoping to catch catfish or trout. In June 1990, a fisherman landed a 2-pound (1-kilogram) black piranha in Cunningham Lake near Omaha, Nebraska. Then in 1994, another fisherman pulled in a 9-inch (23-cm) piranha from Lewis and Clark Lake near Onawa, Iowa. Later, a 13-inch (33-cm) and a 12-inch (30-cm) piranha were caught in a pond just outside of Sioux City, Iowa.

These reports have led some people to wonder how many more piranhas remain in the water if that many have already been caught. Most experts insist that the piranhas that were caught were just a few released pets. But others think that it is unlikely that of all the fish available in these waters, the fishermen just happened to catch these former pets. Some people have begun to wonder if these fish are descendents of the released pets that somehow have adjusted to the temperature change of the water. Could these piranhas be breeding in the waters of the midwestern United States?

Piranhas have fascinated people for hundreds of years. They will become even more fascinating if any more are found in unusual areas.

The experts say that this is impossible. But others are waiting to see how many more piranhas are caught in these unlikely waters.

To Find Out More

Here are some additional resources to help you learn more about piranhas:

 **Books**

Aronsky, Jim. **Crinkleroot's 25 Fish Every Child Should Know.** Bradbury Press, 1993.

Fitzsimons, Cecilia. **Water Life.** Raintree Steck-Vaughn, 1996.

Grossman, Susan. **Piranhas.** Silver Burdett, 1996.

Ling, Mary. **Amazing Fish.** Knopf, 1991.

McAuliffe, Emily. **Piranhas.** Capstone Press, 1997.

Pearce, Q. L. **Piranhas and Other Wonders of the Jungle.** Silver Burdett, 1990.

Organizations and Online Sites

Fish and Wildlife Reference Service
5430 Grosvenor Lane
Suite 110
Bethesda, MD 20814

Index of Aquariums
http://www.aquae.com

Information about public aquariums throughout the world, including those with piranha exhibits.

Piranhas
http://www.piranhas.org

Information including photos, facts about different piranha species, and links to other sites.

Piranha Hut
http://www.piranhahut/index.html

Everything you always wanted to know about piranhas.

Piranha Pages
http://www.pcio.com/piranha

Information about keeping aquarium piranhas, feeding, breeding, species, and more.

Important Words

aquarium large glass tank used to hold fish, small animals, or plants

descendent family member

detect to discover or to find

devour to eat greedily

frenzy frantic, an overly excited state

predator an animal that hunts other animals for food

prey an animal that is hunted by another animal for food

profile side view of the head

school group of fish or other sea creatures

Index

Meet the Author

Elaine Landau has a Bachelor of Arts degree in English and Journalism from New York University and a Masters degree in Library and Information Science from Pratt Institute. She has worked as a newspaper reporter, children's book editor, and a youth services librarian, but especially enjoys writing for young people.

Ms. Landau has written more than one hundred nonfiction books on various topics. She lives in Miami, Florida, with her husband, Norman, and son, Michael.

Photo Credits ©: Aaron Norman: 17, 33 top, 40, 43; Animals Animals: 1 (Miriam Austerman), 11 bottom (Max Gibbs), 4 (Robert Maier), 38 top (Mella Panzella), 11 top (Jack Wilburn); Ben Klaffke: 2, 9, 12, 16, 20, 21, 22 bottom, 28, 31, 33 bottom, 34, 35, 38 bottom; Norbert Wu Photography: 25 (Bob Cranston/Mo Yung Production); Photo Researchers: 29 bottom (Gregory G. Dimijian), 7 (Jacques Jangoux), 26 (Leonide Principe), 22 top (Gary Retherford), 29 top (Alison Wright); John G.Shedd Aquarium: cover, 6, 13 right; Superstock, Inc.: 14; Tony Stone Images: 13 left (Stuart Westmorland); Visuals Unlimited: 36 (G. Prance), 19 (Kjell B. Sandved).
Map by Joe LeMonnier.